Comparing Minibeasts

Minibeast Homes

Charlotte Guillai

B51 089 820 7

KT-144-784

ROTHERHAM LIBRARY SERVICE	
B519820	
Bertrams	22/07/2011
JN	£5.99
CLS	J592.1564

www.raintreepublishers.co.uk
Visit our website to find out
more information about
Raintree books.

To order:
☎ Phone 0845 6044371
🖷 Fax +44 (0) 1865 312263
🖳 Email myorders@raintreepublishers.co.uk

Customers from outside the UK please telephone +44 1865 312262

Raintree is an imprint of Capstone Global Library Limited, a company
incorporated in England and Wales having its registered office at 7 Pilgrim
Street, London, EC4V 6LB – Registered company number: 6695582

Text © Capstone Global Library Limited 2010
First published in hardback in 2010
Paperback edition first published in 2011
The moral rights of the proprietor have been asserted.

All rights reserved. No part of this publication may be reproduced in
any form or by any means (including photocopying or storing it in any
medium by electronic means and whether or not transiently or incidentally
to some other use of this publication) without the written permission of
the copyright owner, except in accordance with the provisions of the
Copyright, Designs and Patents Act 1988 or under the terms of a licence
issued by the Copyright Licensing Agency, Saffron House, 6–10 Kirby Street,
London EC1N 8TS (www.cla.co.uk). Applications for the copyright owner's
written permission should be addressed to the publisher.

Edited by Nancy Dickmann and Catherine Veitch
Designed by Joanna Hinton-Malivoire
Picture research by Elizabeth Alexander
Production by Duncan Gilbert and Victoria Fitzgerald
Originated by Heinemann Library
Printed and bound in China by South China Printing
Company Ltd

ISBN 978 0 431 19492 9 (hardback)
14 13 12 11 10
10 9 8 7 6 5 4 3 2 1

ISBN 978 0 431 19499 8 (paperback)
15 14 13 12 11
10 9 8 7 6 5 4 3 2 1

British Library Cataloguing in Publication Data
Guillain, Charlotte.
Comparing minibeasts.
Homes.
592.1'564-dc22

Acknowledgements
We would would like to thank the following for permission to reproduce
photographs: Alamy pp. **11** (© Roger Eritja), **12** (© Manor Photography),
20 (© Emir Shabashvili), **14** (© cbimages); Capstone Global Library pp. **18**
(Steven Mead), **23 top** (Steven Mead); Corbis pp. **5** (© Theo Allofs/zefa),
16 (© William Radcliffe/Science Faction); FLPA p. **17** (© Konrad Wothe/
Minden Pictures), Photolibrary pp. **4** (Don Johnston/All Canada Photos),
7 (Michael Fogden/OSF), **10** (Oxford Scientific), **8** (Paul Freed/Animals
Animals), **9** (David M Dennis/Animals Animals), **19** (Clarence Styron/age
footstock), **15** (Polka Dot Images), **23 middle bottom** (David M Dennis/
Animals Animals); Shutterstock pp. **6** (© Styve Reineck), **13** (© David Lee),
21 (© Florin Tirlea), **22 top left** (© alle), **22 bottom left** (© Levitskiy
Nikolay), **22 top right** (© aaaah), **22 bottom right** (© Eric Isselée), **23
bottom** (© Florin Tirlea), **23 middle top** (© David Hughes).

Cover photograph of a beehive reproduced with permission of Shutterstock
(©Subbotina Anna). Back cover photograph of termite hills reproduced with
permission of Shutterstock (© Styve Reineck).

The publishers would like to thank Nancy Harris and Kate Wilson for their
assistance in the preparation of this book.

Every effort has been made to contact copyright holders of material
reproduced in this book. Any omissions will be rectified in subsequent
printings if notice is given to the publishers.

Contents

Meet the minibeasts

There are many different types
of minibeasts.

Minibeasts live in many different types of homes.

On and in the ground

Some termites build homes out of mud.

tunnels

Termites make tunnels in their homes.

Some centipedes live in soil.

Earthworms make tunnels in soil.

On water

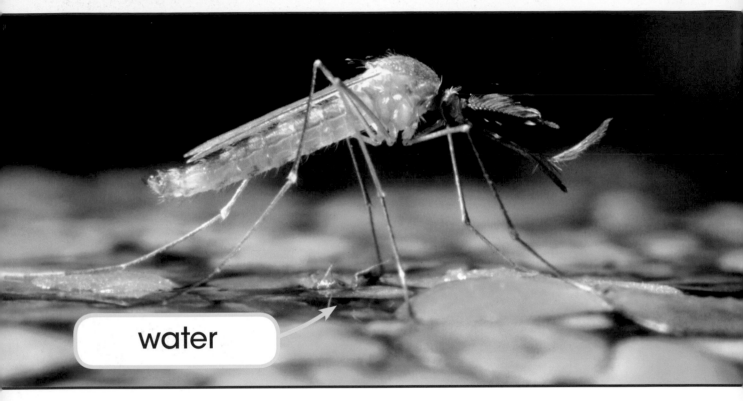

water

Some insects live on water.

eggs

Some insects lay their eggs in water.

Wood

Many insects live in wood.

Many woodlice live under logs.

Plants

leaf

Some insects live on leaves.

stick insect

Some insects live in trees and bushes.

Webs and nests

web

Spiders make webs from silk.

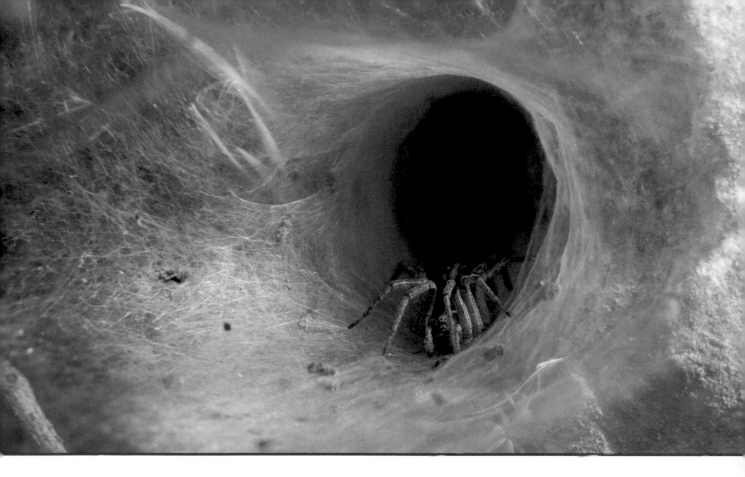

Some spider webs are like tunnels.

nest

Some caterpillars make nests
from silk.

nest

Some wasps make nests from plants they eat.

nest

Honeybees make nests out of wax.

The honeybees live in the nest.

How big?

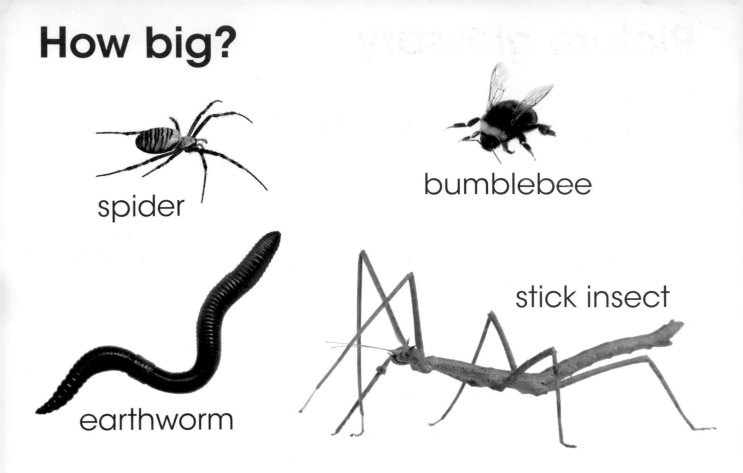

spider

bumblebee

earthworm

stick insect

Look at how big some of the
minibeasts in this book can be.

Picture glossary

silk soft, strong material

soil top layer of ground that you can grow plants in

tunnel long underground passageway

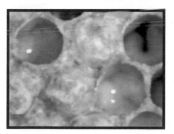

wax sticky yellow material

Index

Notes to parents and teachers

Before reading

Make a list of minibeasts with the children. Try to include insects, arachnids (e.g. spiders), crustaceans (e.g. woodlice), myriapods (e.g. centipedes and millipedes), earthworms, slugs, and snails. Ask the children if they know where any of these minibeasts live. What sort of homes do minibeasts make for themselves?

After reading

- Go on a hunt for spider webs – a good time to do this is on a misty morning. Where do spiders make their webs? Take photographs of the webs you find and look at them together on the interactive whiteboard. Look at the structure of the webs carefully. Try making a web together with string on the classroom wall. Is this easy to do?
- Take the children to hunt for other minibeasts. Help them to peel back bark on rotten logs, look under stones, look for worms in soil, or find caterpillars on leaves. Draw up tally charts with the children to record how many different places minibeasts were found.
- Read the children *The Very Busy Spider* by Eric Carle.